What Cl

"My time with Ruth Mott has been one of the most defining experiences of my entire life. When I finally write the book on everything I've slogged through to get resituated at the midlife of my career, it'll be dedicated to Ruth Mott."

—JOHN VIEHMAN, MAGAZINE PUBLISHER, MAINE

"Ruth challenged me, guided me but most of all believed in me. She helped me believe in myself as well."

—MARK DEAN, U.S. NATIONAL SALES MANAGER, ELECTRICAL MANFACTURING COMPANY, CANADA

"Ruth takes a no-nonsense approach to *bringing out and sharpening my strengths.* She has enabled me to realize *more of my potential* to lead, communicate and create."

—ALLAN COHEN, GLOBAL INDEPENDENT CONSULTANT

"Working with Ruth allowed me to learn more about myself. With her knowledge and sharp business sense (she) always made me feel comfortable and confident with my decisions."

—CRAIG GOLDSTEIN, VICE-PRESIDENT, INTERNATIONAL BANKING CO., NY

"Working with Ruth has not only changed my work style and effectiveness as a senior manager, but she has become my conscience."

—Frank Maniaci, Director, International Investment Bank, N.Y.

"With Ruth's help you can expect to become more effective, confident and successful in any areas you wish to improve... and maybe some you didn't even know you wanted to work on."

—JASON WALL, TECHNOLOGY CONSULTANT, NEW HAMPSHIRE

"Ruth doesn't pull any punches, tells it like it is and can help you get where you want to go!"

—LYNNE DONNELLY, CST, EFTCERT-II

"In a few sessions ... Ruth's coaching helped me land the job of my dreams! *Thanks Ruth.*"

—NATHAN LEVENSON, MANAGING DIRECTOR,
EDUCATION MANAGEMENT COUNCIL

"Ruth challenged me to move *outside the lines of traditional corporate behavior,* and to view myself through a different lens."

—ANNETTE TONTI, CEO OF MOFUSE,
MOBIL CONTENT MANAGEMENT

"I will not make an important decision, I will not go to a critical meeting without first polling Ruth for her thoughts."

—MATTHEW LAMPROS, CEO, SELLEMENTAL.COM

I Love You—
Now Get Over
Yourself!

7 Secrets
for Professional Success from
The Jewish Mother Executive Coach

Ruth B. Mott

Frontpiece

"When I was asked by the nurse in the emergency room what my blood type was, I realized I didn't know it so I called my mother to find out. She said, "Well, your blood type is B+ but if you had listened to me, you would have an A!" *And that, my friends, is a Jewish Mother!'*

—MARK GOODMAN, RUTH'S SON, AND
A SUCCESSFUL CHOREOGRAPHER, PERFORMER AND TEACHER

Table of Contents

Foreword

I'll never forget the day I first met Ruth Mott. I had recently taken on a position as a speech coach and editor at Index Consulting, the company that flowered and faded with the re-engineering boom and bust in the 90s. It wasn't Day One, but it was Week One. I was still meeting people at a great clip, and most of their names went in one overwhelmed ear and out the other, but there was something different about Ruth that you didn't forget.

Ruth fixes you with a look that is completely 'present', as the actors say, and suddenly the meaning of the day is on notice. *Better make this good*, I thought first, and then, *who* is *this woman?* I vaguely resented her in the next instant, because somehow I knew she expected a lot from me. But why me? And why a lot? What did I owe her?

Ruth manages to communicate all this within the first minute of meeting her, you see, and she has a way of suddenly opening up your world with possibilities by the questions she asks and those looks she gives you, as if to say, *well? What do you have for me? What do you have to say for yourself?*

Does it go without saying that she manages all this with a twinkle in her eye, so that you know that whatever happens will also be fun?

Ruth and I have known each other for something like fifteen years now, maybe a little more. And we've worked on screenplays, joint coaching projects, and conferences galore. All of them have been eye-opening, mind-expanding, and fun. So when she told me she was writing a book I naturally thought to myself, *well? What do you have for me? What do you have to say for yourself?*

Read this book, because it distills some of the wisdom from a remarkable woman indeed. It's indeed a pleasure to turn the question tables on Ruth and ask her, *what do you have to say for yourself?* – because of course the answer is, a great deal packed into a modest-sized space. And all of it will push you to think in new ways, to take the measure of yourself, and to do yourself a little prouder.

Nick Morgan, Ph.D.
Founder, Publicwords.com

Acknowledgements

Others have helped every successful person toward their success. Me too. As I was making this list, I began to think about each of them in depth. What a fortunate person I am to have such wonderful, generous, graceful, intelligent, humorous, unselfish people in my life! Wow.

First, I want to acknowledge all my clients. Allowing me to help guide you through your varied journeys is a gift. I learned so much from each of you, whether long-term or a "one-night stand". Thank you for bestowing me with your trust.

I thank the brilliant Nick Morgan for his thoughtful and intelligent editing of this book. He pushed me to answer hard questions, helped me to dig deeper inside myself to offer up something useful. Nick is an author, an internationally recognized coach, a speaker, a colleague, and a friend. And the epitome of a **"mentsh"** (a truly admirable person)! Reading **his** books will make you better at everything.

To those I am about to name, I am truly grateful for your support, your honesty, and your belief in me. You are all inspirations and consummate professionals. You all have shown a lot of courage to withstand my **"meshugass"** – that means my craziness – my kvetching, my self-pitying, my crises of confidence, my chutzpah. And you did it all lovingly. At least, it felt that way. There is quite obviously some Jewish Mother in each of you.

Because the help that each of you gave me was so critical to whatever next step I had to take, I am listing your names in alphabetical order (by last name). No matter where your name falls, it is there because I needed your wisdom. Thank you:

Dave Burke, Allan Cohen, Ron Donovan, Janice Eddy, Lenny Fogel, Alan Foster, Matthew Lampros, Henry Osti, Ann Overton, Helene Richter, Peter Rogovin, Annette Tonti, Tedd Tramaloni, Niki Vettel, John Viehman, Larry Wegman.

To my good friends who cheered me on in this highly questionable pursuit, thank you for your support and love:

Lucy Borodkin, Shirley Coburn, Lynne Donnelly, Barbara Franzoso, Wendy Frosh, Amanda Hickman, Lisa Hirsh, Andy Livingston, Maxine Morse, DB Reiff, Donna Ryan, Eliza "Pippa" Shulman, Jodi Sperber, Cullen Spiller.

And to my two offspring, Laura and Mark, who didn't know whether to ask for a psych evaluation or just wish me luck, thank you for secretly being proud of me. They think I'm a **"bissel meshugeh"** (a little nuts), but they kept it under control and never "dissed" my efforts.

Introduction

I'm Ruth Mott and I'm an executive coach. I'm also a Jewish mother.

You know the typical Jewish Mother. We always have something to say on every topic and we're not shy about saying it. We also can embody wisdom, honesty, and caring. Most of all, we can laugh at you and with you, and remain your best friend whose only concern is your success.

That's me in a paragraph.

I've been a coach for 18 years and a Jewish Mother for many more than that. What have I learned from all that? I coach like I live: direct, insistent, with a touch of guilt and a lot of love.

Yes, love is the most important ingredient of my coaching. Sound schmaltzy? Maybe, but it is the truth. Early in life I learned that no matter what I did (and I did some pretty dicey things), my parents would still love me, after they got done letting me know that they were angry, disappointed, and ashamed of my behavior. Through it all, I was loved. That's the essential piece that gave me the courage to try many things and take many risks. Asking and helping people to take risks requires that they feel safe, admired – and loved.

Of course, not every client loves me, and certainly not all the time. Some of them don't at all. But I love them!

OK – so some a little more than others, but I love them all to some degree. As a consequence, they feel safe, relieved and empowered and that is why they are successful.

If we could sit down together with a cup of coffee, maybe a cheese Danish, and talk, I'd get to hear your concerns, experiences, and opinions. And, of course, offer my advice. But since we can't do that, and too much cheese Danish clogs your arteries, I have written this little book based on the seven most frequent issues clients bring to me. Here you will find clarity around many of the personal issues you deal with in your professional lives everyday. Use it as a guide to help you think about and solve the problems facing you. (If you do what I tell you, you wll be so much better off.)

Of course, as I said, I wouldn't be a Jewish Mother coach if I didn't sprinkle all that love with a little bit of guilt every now and then. In my practice, I hold clients accountable for their own commitment to their own success. Because I'm not literally holding your hand or making you feel just a little bit guilty, YOU have to do it – hold yourself accountable for your own success. This little book will help you do that.

To my clients, I promise you that your situation has not been singled out. Each scenario is based on many different situations with similar aspects. All of you have served as teachers for me and now get to serve as teachers for others who face the same issues you confronted and mastered.

In this book you will find how you put one foot in front of the other to reach the next level of whatever journey you're on. If you take your Jewish Mother coach with you, **of course you'll be successful**! Trust me. Would I lie to you?

"The best way to predict your future is to create it"
—*Abraham Lincoln*

Chapter 1

On the One Hand This on the Other Hand That

What If I Make the Wrong Choice?

YOU HAVE CHOICES – MAZEL TOV!

So it's crunch time and you have to choose a direction for your next career move and it's scaring the hell out of you. Of course it is.

You're thinking, *What if I make the wrong choice?* Well, they could all be wrong choices. Welcome to real life. On the other hand they could all be right choices. Oy vey, what a dilemma!

Here's the good news:

∾ ↶

Having choices – even not so great ones – is a sign of success. Whatever you've been doing has led you to the place you are now - in a position to make a move of some kind. Good work!

∾ ↶

Making a choice that may affect the rest of your life requires courage and a leap of faith. That's hard. You'll naturally think of all the worst-case scenarios – all of the things that could go wrong. You may be frozen like a cold potato latke, or a deer in the indecision headlights. Some of that thinking is helpful – you don't want to pick blindly. But at some point you have to, well, get off the pot.

So what do you do? You seek the opinion of every friend, every acquaintance and maybe even strangers on the subway. While you may get some interesting feedback and even some ideas you hadn't thought of from all that reaching out, what it really does is keep you smack in the middle of the dilemma.

We all do it. And we all sometimes fail to make a choice until something forces us to, or we reluctantly choose one of the alternatives. Many of us don't make any choice at all and stay in the present situation waiting for the next best thing. This is **"nisht gut"** (not such a good thing). It's a vicious circle.

The longer you agonize over the advantages and disadvantages of each alternative, the longer you delay your future. Each of the alternatives presents opportunities and choosing one over the other has its benefits and drawbacks. So how do you step off?

DON'T EXAMINE YOUR CHOICES FIRST, EXAMINE YOUR HOPE

The best way to approach any decision is to look at your HOPE first and *then* the **choices**. And the best way to do that is by **SAYING OUT LOUD WHAT YOU REALLY WANT. And then write it down.**

Do you want a particular job, a particular salary, celebrity status, a job that lets you wear jeans every day – or all of the above?

I always ask my clients, if I could wave a magic wand and give you the two things you really want tomorrow, what would they be? **Then I ask, how much are you willing to risk to get those things?**

When you ask yourself these questions and you answer them honestly, you may surprise yourself.

RISKY BUSINESS

Making a choice that will affect your future life is most certainly a risk and it does take courage. This is why what *you **hope for yourself** has to be your guide for the choices you make in life.* If you're going to be risking that much, make it on something worthwhile!

Sometimes the choices presented to you are not what you would have asked for or are not so swell. But your *hope* for your life **IS** the right guide.

When you have examined your hope and matched the alternatives as closely as possible to the desired outcome, then lay out your plan to get there. What things do you have to do to get to that goal?

❧ ❧

Staying in the dilemma will give you heartburn.
Making a decision may also give you heartburn,
but it will give you a direction, which is better
than staying in flux.

❧ ❧

Be careful. Sometimes you find that the choices you have don't come close to the hope you have for yourself. This is altogether a different problem. Chapter 2 will help you with that one.

There was a time in my life when, though I had a good job, I wanted more. I wanted to be a famous producer of documentary films. (Yes, famous! Why not?) An opportunity presented itself. I had to take a major leap of faith – and quit my good job – to pursue that hope.

Well, I didn't become the filmmaker I had envisioned, but I did work in television for a few years and absolutely loved it! I knew I had staked a claim for my hope and while it didn't give me everything, it gave me the opportunity to learn, to work with creative and talented people, and provided experiences I never would have had if I hadn't made the leap. Those were many of the things I had written on my "what do I really want" list.

❧ ❧

Sometimes life circumstances do not afford us great choices. For example being compelled to keep a job because we need the money and it's too risky to try something else. If you have good choices, it's a "mitzvah" (a blessing) be grateful because many people don't, or think they don't.

Chapter 1
Client Story

Marilyn

Marilyn was a senior manager faced with having to make a difficult choice in a difficult economy. She was downsized.

At first she was upset and scared, of course. She was her own sole source of support and needed to work to live. But Marilyn was a gutsy woman. She went back and forth between being scared and being excited because she saw it as an opportunity to move back to where she truly wanted to live. She saw the choice as one between familiarity and starting over.

Staying in the area had many advantages. Friends, professional recognition, a nice house – life in the comfort zone. Moving to her preferred place meant having to build that all over again.

She had a little money and a small severance package. She knew she could collect unemployment, so she did have breathing room to make her decision.

Her daily mental muddle went like this: "On the one hand, I can stay with what I know even though I'm unhappy here. On the other hand I could move to where I really want to live and take the chance that I will get a job – even in this economy." She kept going in circles. She asked every friend, every acquaintance what they thought, and stayed firmly entrenched in the middle of her dilemma.

When I pushed her (from many directions), what became clear was that she really wanted to live in her preferred place. That represented happiness. In fact, she wanted it so much that she was sabotaging her chances of finding a job where she was presently living. She applied for jobs and had interviews but somehow found ways to undermine her candidacy. She was surprised to see what she was doing when I confronted her with it, but admitted the truth of it.

So we looked at HOW Marilyn could realize her hope of moving to her preferred place. She would have to pay a hefty sum to get out of a lease. Moving costs were very high, and renting a place would also be expensive. She was quickly going through her severance. She had enough to last 2-3 months at the rate she was going.

So we developed a plan and a realistic financial approach that gave her the resources she needed for at least six months. That meant doing some negotiating with her present landlord, finding a moving company that was reasonable and staying with a friend for a while.

There was suddenly a lot to do. She had to have her resume done. She had to identify the 5 companies she thought she would like to work for in the new area. She had to use LinkedIn to see if she had any connections to the identified companies. She had to make the phone calls, send the e-mails, and arrange the move.

But what a difference in her attitude and effort! Instead of going in circles, she put her energies to the task of moving to her preferred place. It wasn't going to be easy and it wasn't going to happen within a week, but it was going to happen.

She did move, and she had a really hard time finding a job, but she did find one in the end. And it was worth the fear, the effort, and the stress because she was where she wanted to be.

IF YOU ARE LUCKY ENOUGH TO BE DEALING WITH CHOICES, HERE IS YOUR JEWISH MOTHER'S COACHING ADVICE:

1. Say out loud what you really want. Listen to yourself.

2. Write down what you really want.

3. Then examine the choices to see which one gives you or might give you what you really want – or comes the closest.

4. Be honest about what you can tolerate – but don't be a wuss. So it's hard, scary, whatever – these are your dreams, right?

5. Work out the steps you will need to get it. Just like Marilyn, figure out if you need to contact friends; and make appointments to talk to people. Start putting your energy toward actually GETTING what you say you want.

6. Then start, already! Once you begin moving in the direction of your hopes, you will create great energy and you will be ACTING in your own interest instead of talking about it.

P.S. Often we need someone to hold our hands when we make decisions. If you do, find a coach – or a friend – who will guide and encourage you through the process.

On the other hand, sometimes a good hot pastrami sandwich is enough to get you through!

"You're through. Finished. Burned out. Used up.
You've been replaced, forgotten. That's a lie!"
—Charles R. Swindoll

Chapter 2

I Just Don't Have It Anymore!

Crisis Of Confidence

OH MAN! I THINK I'M IN THE WRONG BUSINESS

Do you love what you're doing? Did you ever love what you're doing? Why did you choose what you're doing? Did it choose you?

A crisis of confidence is one of the most common issues my clients present to me. Successful people hit a wall, and then start to doubt themselves. It feels like everything they've done doesn't matter and they can't see the future anymore. Everything is a chore, they're tired all the time, and they feel guilty, and secretly scared they will lose everything.

The thought process goes something like this: I just don't have it anymore; I'm too old; I'm burned out. If you say that long enough, you'll start to believe it.

So now what? Here's the surprise:

A CRISIS OF CONFIDENCE IS A SIGN OF SUCCESS

A crisis of confidence hits you when whatever you've been doing up to a certain point has been working just fine and then NOT! You may start doing something you've never done and so begin to doubt your abilities. Or perhaps you're so busy doing what needs to get done you forget why you're doing it at all and you burn out. Or maybe you actually decide to change direction and then scare yourself to death with the prospect. You may find yourself **"kvetching"** (complaining) a lot.

Now I know that there are other crises of confidence that come from very dire circumstances and not necessarily from success. You might face extremely difficult financial circumstances, or find yourself beaten down by life in general. These are real and terrible, and this advice is not for those moments.

But when you think you're burned out, washed up, and no longer good at your job, it may be that you are in the wrong line of work, and your soul has finally caught up with your occupation. On the other hand, it may be that you need to reconnect with your passion for what you're doing, or at least, the reason you're doing it. If you want to take a new direction and it's a **"bissel"** (little) terrifying, remember Chapter I – examine your hope first.

It is so easy to give in to feelings of inadequacy when you're in the midst of such a crisis. It's difficult to think clearly. It's frightening and it can destroy careers, friendships, or even marriages. It's debilitating and often very difficult to come out of. But that doesn't mean it can't be overcome. Not at all.

In fact, a crisis of confidence is a healthy thing. I know that seems like a contradiction. But dealt with properly

It forces you to examine your behaviors and to ask yourself questions about why you're doing what you're doing. And that's a good thing.

A crisis of confidence CAN help you regain your conscious awareness of why you chose your profession at all. What did you want from it? What do you get from it? What do you bring to the table?

THE BIG PIECE HERE:

You need to acknowledge your success so you can reconnect with your passion, or whatever reason brought you to your work in the first place!

(BTW – these are the questions to ask yourself if, in Chapter I, you find your choices have nothing to do with your hope.)

Personally, I've had several crises of confidence in my life. The latest was when I decided to write this book. I whined, moaned, made several attempts and hit the same brick wall every time. "Nothing I have to say is important or of any value." What a way to talk! I've been successfully coaching people for a long time and I couldn't connect that with putting it in a book – even a little book. My big hope was to help as many people as I could. Whining got me nothing. So, I got a coach, I took a course, and just started doing it. Is it easy - No - but where is it written that it should be easy? Is it scary – yes – but that's when you know it's worth doing.

Chapter 2
Client Story

Jarrod

Jarrod was a marketing executive who found himself in a downward spiral of no energy, no interest, and no confidence. Up to this point, he had been quite successful and loved his work. He loved it from the very beginning, having made the conscious decision to do this work, but now he was unsure. His desire was gone. He felt his work was mediocre at best and therefore not serving clients. He said to himself, "I just don't have it anymore."

What was really happening was that Jarrod's success was starting to get in the way of doing what he really loved about his work. A contradiction? Not so much!

His agency was successful, but it was hit hard by the recession and he had to downsize. He did that by letting go some of the support staff. Jarrod found himself having to do much of the clerical work – bookkeeping, billing, hiring administrative support, and other back and front office issues that he hated. He was not doing enough of the creative work that he loved. He got so worn down that he was unable to focus on the creative side of his job. He was in that downward spiral of *I'm not doing what I love, I'm so tired, I don't have it any more, I'm washed up.*

We had to get Jarrod to the place where he could remember why he chose his profession in the first place – what he wanted from it, what he got from it, what he brought to the table. Then, he needed to acknowledge his success so that he could reconnect with his passion for his work.

First we talked about why he chose his profession. Was this THE thing he wanted to do? What did he love about it, and what special talents did he bring to it? As we talked, he got very animated, the juices started to flow, and he got nostalgic about what it used to be like – as he claimed. As we went through this process, Jarrod could feel the fire in the belly returning – something he'd been missing for quite awhile.

To help him hang on to those feelings we had to build a support for them – like a scaffolding –that would allow him to access his passion at will. The solution was not very glamorous. It didn't need to be, it just had to effective.

We devised a schedule that deliberately built in time for both creativity and the necessary clerical work.

He needed 3 things: 1) undisturbed thinking time for creative thinking and strategy development; 2) time for his own head clearing which he got from working out at the gym; and 3), even though it was his least favorite thing, he needed time for the clerical activities he had to handle.

Blocking out time for Jarrod's tasks – all 3 of them - was the key to helping him feel he had control of his days. He kept two half-days when he was not to be disturbed to do the things he loved most: strategy development for his clients and creating pitches for potential clients.

Of course, creative work has to be done all the time, but on the days when he was putting out fires, or other priorities competed for his attention, he knew he had at least 8 hours when he would be able to focus on the things he loved most.

We also blocked out time for him to get to the gym – 7-8 am 4 days a week. And yes, a few hours in the morning to do the clerical stuff.

It wasn't that he was washed up. He was overwhelmed and in conflict with his own desires. This caused emotional and physical exhaustion, which led him to believe he was burnt out and that he didn't have it anymore. He was smack-dab in the middle of a crisis of confidence not because he couldn't do it anymore, but because he had been doing it very well and wanted it to continue that way. But circumstances changed and he had to roll with it. He lost touch with what he loved and had to recover his passion.

If you're having a crisis of confidence here is Your Jewish Mother's Coaching Advice:

These are the things I tell my clients to do. They do them and they work. They will work for you too.

1. Don't whine. Remember a crisis of confidence is a sign of success. It means everything has worked so far.

2. Ask yourself the following questions:

   a) Why am I in the game at all?
   b) What do I love about it?

If you can't come up with anything, you're in the wrong business and have to start looking more deeply for what does inspire you.

3. What is the job giving you and what are you giving it?

4. Are you giving your job your best talents?

5. What are you doing for yourself to HELP you do the job? Reading books, taking courses, getting feedback?

6. Are you taking time to exercise to keep your body in good shape?

7. Are you taking time to stop and smell the flowers to keep your spirit and your mind in good shape?

If you say, yeah, I know all this, but doing it is another thing. I know, I get it, but it's still a copout. If you can't see yourself doing all of it, pick one! **Just start.**

*"The secret of life is honesty and fair dealing.
If you can fake that, you've got it made!"*
—Groucho Marx

Chapter 3

Put On A Little Makeup, No One Will Know

What If They Find Out I'm a Fake?

WHO DO YOU THINK YOU ARE ANYWAY?

The story you buy about yourself comes from your past – your failures, your successes, things people tell you at vulnerable moments. Maybe you always have that little voice that says "lucky break," even in the midst of success, meaning you just got lucky. And, if you keep holding on to such a story, your colleagues, friends, and family will come to believe it.

Maybe you're someone who has a very strong ego and refused to buy into any of the negative stuff you got in the past. If so, congratulations – you don't need to read any further. At least not in this chapter. This chapter is for those who bought into the dumb luck myth even just a little bit.

You often don't try for a position you want because you're afraid you don't have anything to bring to the table. Or you find yourself doing the best you can and hope no one finds out that you're making it up as you go along. Your middle-of-the-night goblins taunt you with the fear that someone will see the obvious and tell others that you are really counterfeit. Well, the fact is:

Your experiences are multifaceted and give you knowledge and sophistication applicable in many different areas. You just have to be creative about how to adapt those experiences to the next challenge.

For example, if you're a financial advisor you know how to do research, you know how to create budgets, and you know how to analyze data. Therefore, you can say with confidence that, while you have not been head of a field study group, you have skills to be part of such a group.

If you have been helping people organize and prioritize their work load, coaching others on how to ask for something they need, resolving conflicts, helping people see the big picture, working toward compromise – then people trust you. Of course you can run for office!

Here's the takeaway:

∽ ∾

Look at the things you've done and develop a broader view of all the talents you used to be successful.

∽ ∾

You also need to be realistic. If you are unable to ask for things that people may not want to give, then being in a command position may not be right for you. Overselling will lead to failure and, of course, you <u>will</u> feel counterfeit.

∽ ∾

As you enlarge your view of your experience, and then creatively apply those attributes to other areas, you will see that indeed you are not counterfeit – your journey was just a bit different.

∽ ∾

You have the right to bring your skills to the table.

25

Chapter 3

Client Story:

LOREN

After several years of being a successful in-house sales manager, Loren was moving from one area of the country to another. She accepted a position as Director of Business Development in a mid-sized firm. When she was interviewed for the job, she made a great impression and convinced the hiring manager that in her former position as sales manager, business development was a hat she had to wear because the firm was small and everyone had to take on several roles.

The only problem was that her business development experience was really very limited and then only as an add-on to her sales position. For example, if she was selling to a company she also tried to recruit that company to become a larger client than they originally signed on for.

Therefore, she saw herself as a fraud and began to undermine her own abilities and successes. When she called me she was panicking.

First, we looked at her experience. Her professional experience included selling, developing successful business plans, bookkeeping, and designing marketing programs. Her volunteer experience included heading the Major Gifts Committee for a medical care organization, which meant she had to ask businesses in the community for large sums of money. She did that by convincing them that the work of the non-profit was important to the community at large and gave the major donors wonderful exposure as good corporate citizens.

Now nowhere in that experience is the title 'Business Developer'. But the skills it took for her to be successful taught her

1. How to approach a client with the right story
2. How to talk about finances and the value of doing business with her
3. How to help people understand the ROI of doing business with her organization
4. How to make the connections between a client's business objectives and whatever she was selling

Her middle-of-the-night goblins were telling her she just didn't have it. They were telling her that she lied her way in and that as soon as someone found it out she would be exposed and banished.

Here's the deal. We all have goblins – particularly in the middle of the night. When we go out on a limb by making bold statements and opening ourselves up for criticisms or being stripped naked, we start to believe we really are frauds. The goblins come from our pasts from people telling us we couldn't, wouldn't, or shouldn't.

We have to allow the goblins to have their time. Then, we get up in the morning, and move on. If you're struggling, look at your past experiences again, and verify that while you don't know everything, you do know enough to do a good job. Everything we have done lends itself to doing something else. We acquire skills that help us do the next thing.

The only thing Loren lacked was a previous title of Business Developer. So what's so terrible? She has it now and she is doing a great job.

Your Experience is Light? – Not to Worry

So what does it mean if you only have a few things to examine regarding your experience? Simple – it means that you still have stuff to think about and repurpose toward some other professional activity. AND, it means that maybe you're not ready yet for the particular job you're trying to land. So, you need to think about that career track, what job you COULD take to get more experience toward the end goal and go for that. This is a journey, one that flows, not a dead end!

For example, I had a client who wanted to be in on-line advertising. Her experience was as a production manager in television. She could sell her experience of creating and maintaining budgets, vetting, hiring, and supervising crews, creating, managing and controlling traffic, but she didn't have the on-line experience. Because she had those experiences she was able to get a job - at less salary than she originally wanted - as a junior traffic manager in a large ad agency. She already knew video inside and out, but she learned about print, about on-line banners, and other things necessary for the job she wanted and eventually got.

This is sometimes what it takes. Whatever you can come up with in terms of what you do know and to creatively think about how that applies elsewhere is a plus. If you don't have lots, **you do have some**. Don't whine. Use it as a guide to your next professional adventure.

Goblins and Monsters and Demons, Oh My!

In Shakespeare's Macbeth, the Hags (witches) brew up the cauldron of toil and trouble by throwing in all kinds of goblin-like things, hedge-pigs, eyes of newts, owls wings – all kinds of **"chazzerei"** (junk).

This is what we all do during that long midnight hour when we are haunted by the list of shortcomings – those goblins or demons we think we have. This activity borne of our own insecurities serves no purpose but to take us to the place of ineptness, guilt, and failure. Like the Hags, it is our own entire brew.

When we finally wake for the day, we may shake off those goblins but you can be sure they are still lurking. We all have them, in one form or another, and for some of us, they scare us silly. Mind you, there is always a kernel of truth in them – but the trick is to remember that it is only a kernel. Our subconscious takes over, causing the cauldron of our lives to boil over. Remember the phrase from Walt Kelly and Pogo? - "We have met the enemy, and it is us."

I don't have any great tricks to teach you about how to overcome these goblins. But in true Jewish Mother Tradition, I do have advice – good advice, tried and true.

You need to look at them in the bright light of day and, if you can, put them in perspective – make them into kernels - actually picture them in your own mind as kernels of corn – name it, and put it away. Will it silence them? Not completely. But you can keep them at bay by recognizing two things: most of us have goblins AND we are responsible for their existence. We can control them to a degree by recognizing that they come from a place of fear and old stories.

See them for what they really are. You are the driver of how much they influence your view of yourself. Moreover, you are the one who sees yourself in that way and you need to be careful not to lay that on others.

If the demons are many and at a deep level, you may need the help of a therapist. One thing I know, however, and this is true for everyone, if you don't acknowledge them, they will sabotage every thing you try to do.

1. First, recognize that everyone has goblins of some kind. You are not alone.

2. Do a little self-analysis. Examine each of the positions you've held over the past 2-5 years and list what talents you had to use to do the job successfully. Use the examples in the chapter as guides.
   On a scale of 1-5, rate yourself as to how successfully you used each of these talents. 1 is not so good, 5 is great!

3. Group your answers – put all 1s together, 2s, and so on. Talents have multiple applications.
   Remember, you are not trying to say you are an *expert* in all areas, but the talents you have in one place are useful in other places as well.

4. Get some help with this if you have to. There are coaches, career counselors, mentors, everywhere and their job is to help you recognize that your experience and talents are transferable to many undertakings.

*"Winners regroup whenever necessary
on the path to winning."*
—*Seth Godin*

Chapter 4

What Do You Mean You Didn't Get A Speaking Part?

Separate Me From The Pack!

RAZZLE-DAZZLE 'EM! – WHAT DIFFERENCE DID YOU MAKE?

You want to get an award. You want to get a promotion. You want to get a grant. You want to be selected over everyone else for something that hundreds (thousands, or maybe just the final 3) are vying for. Good luck!

The way to get noticed is by standing out. And the way to do that is by continually asking yourself – and answering – this question:

∽ ∾

What difference did it make that I was there?

∽ ∾

If you did a good job, no one will notice you. They may not even notice you if you did a great job. But they **will** take notice if you did something outstanding. The real trick:

∽ ∾

Make your accomplishment look,
sound and feel outstanding

∽ ∾

I don't mean lying about it. I mean creatively pointing out the difference that **your** solution, **your** production, **your** outcome, made. Often, the best way to accomplish this is to get someone else to praise the difference you made.

For example, when I worked in Public Television we won an award for the most creative Pledge Drive (when stations ask the public to become members). The way we applied for the award was to talk about how it influenced the viewers, of course, bringing in more members than we had last time out. But we talked about how it influenced the *staff* of the station as well. A pledge drive takes many, many, hours to produce and to put on. We would be at the station from 8 in the morning until midnight for 17 days with barely time to breathe. Writing and rewriting pledge "spots" for the on-air talent to deliver. And most often, the on-air-talent were not trained professionals. They were people from the community.

In our submission we talked about the numbers – all increasing by such-and-such an amount or percentage. But we also talked about how much fun the drive was for us, for our "talent" and for the community at large and got quotes from viewers testifying to the fun. It was a very creative drive, if I do say so myself, but every station thinks they produce a creative drive. What made our submission remarkable? The razzle and the dazzle was the testimony from viewers. They proclaimed that the drive was outstanding, and that made our case.

What Have You Done For Them Lately?

Sometimes it means you talk about what the consequences would have been if you hadn't done what you did. For example, by putting a new process in place, your company avoided a major loss of some kind. Creative thinking, changing a strategy, taking a risk, resulted in _____. Fill in the blank. And it's all because you were there.

❧ ❧

It's all about outcomes. Let me repeat, it's all about outcomes.

❧ ❧

When you ask yourself, "what difference did it make that I was there," answer it in terms of outcomes. How was it better because it was you and not someone else?

Please do not confuse this with bragging. The difference is that you are telling your story to help others see how you have contributed and to see your value. Bragging is just singing your own praises with no concern for how others benefited. So be truthful, but own your success. You want to be a humble **"macher'** (someone who makes a difference).

Standing out means standing up for yourself. It is about stepping into your talents and telling the preeminent story of who you are, what difference you've made in your profession, in the lives of others, and in the organizations you work for.

Sometimes it's hard to quantify the outcome. It requires creativity to show that things were truly better because you were there. If you didn't make any difference, then there's no reason to think about you any differently than anyone else. But you can razzle-dazzle 'em if you try.

If you are constantly telling people how great you are because you've accomplished something, well, nobody likes a showoff! And, you lose whatever credibility you might have.

If you're constantly telling people how much you have done for the organization – this too is not a good thing. Nobody likes a showoff!

If you are being asked either formally or informally (writing a submission for an award, for an off the cuff opinion, or seriously asked how to accomplish something) then it's easier to be brilliant and show off your ideas. Still, you want them to be thoughtful and useful so that others will take you seriously.

The best way to spotlight your intelligence when you're not being asked specifically, is three-fold:

1. **Ask a question**
2. Be prepared to argue (debate, defend, discuss) your reasoning
3. Be open to whatever criticism you encounter and agile enough to incorporate feedback.

When you are not being asked and you have some good ideas, that's a good time to show how and why it's cool – even important - that you're there. By asking questions first, you will have a much more willing ear.

Whether it's something the organization has been grappling with and you have a good idea about how to change it, or you are being proactive and can see a better way to do things, bring it to your staff meeting, bring it to your boss at your one-on-one, or take her out for coffee.

Questions such as: I'd like your opinion. Or, what do you think about doing it this way? Or, I'm thinkin' it might work better if we do… what do you think? Or, I'd like to try doing. ., because it will give us better…..

Make sure you are asking the questions
of the right person.

That is, your boss, your VP, the CEO, another manager, someone who has a stake in listening and not someone

39

who will be interested so much in stealing your idea. Ideally it should be someone who will be as interested in the *fact thatYOU had the idea* as well as how it works for the organization.

How Do I Do It If We're All at a Bar Mitzvah?

While it's easy to do this in the office, it is a little more difficult to do this in social situations such as a business cocktail party or dinner. Normally, I would advise you not to do it at all. But the Big Boss is in town and this is the only opportunity you may have to talk with her. You really feel you have to make a move now.

Subtlety and strategy are the most important elements here. If you are not practiced or particularly good at this – don't do it. It may really offend your listener and that conduct could damage your career for good. Wait for the next workday, the next celebration, or an opportunity to do something business-wide that the BB is sure to know about. However, if you think you can do it successfully, then give it a try.

Even if you are good at it, remember, the best way to let someone know that you are a star is to first **ask** how things are going. Then tell them you've been thinking about whatever it is and you have some thoughts on how to **"increase" "decrease" "advance"** it that you would like to discuss. These are key words that heighten curiosity, use them. It needs to be about them and/or the business and not about you.

Be prepared with a short pithy answer to a question you might be asked and the answer should include how it benefits the organization. Such as "I think it will save the company $$$" (you get the idea). If the person wants to talk about it then, fine, go ahead. Otherwise simply say you will call them in the morning and set up a meeting. Be sure to add, "I really think this will help us to...." Or something that shows your confidence in your idea.

∽ ∾

Your own conviction about your idea is what will peak the interest of others.

∽ ∾

Do not do this with every cockamamie idea you have. It has to count, so be as sure as you can be that it actually moves the organization forward, or it is a new and more efficient way to do what you already do, or it will save money. Pretty soon you will be seen as a "person of interest", maybe even a **"maven"** (an expert). You WILL get a speaking part and your star will rise!

Chapter 4

Client Story

RICHARD

Reaching for the next level, Richard needed an "edge." Something that would make him stand out from the crowd. And, believe me, there was quite a crowd vying for the position of VP for Project Management.

So how did we help him stand out? Simple. We asked what difference he made in his previous – and present – positions. Just detailing his many responsibilities without showing what impact he had would throw him in the hat with everyone else. Our task was to make his candidacy sparkle.

Part of the problem was that Richard's job didn't lend itself easily to quantifying outcomes. That is, we couldn't say he saved the company xxx amount of money. But we could say it indirectly.

Richard was a project manager; he managed processes. Merely saying that all processes ran smoothly under his management isn't very exciting. So we analyzed his workday. As it turns out, he was able to keep every project on time and on budget, eliminating costly overtime and avoiding unhappy clients. The difference: the year before he was hired the company spent $$$ in outsourcing, hiring temps, and lost 2 clients.

Richard came in and:

1. put accountability standards in place for the various teams;
2. negotiated a stricter contract with the outsourcers;
3. and had a daily "hot list" outlining what had to be accomplished that day.

The outcomes included:

- 150% less overtime – saving a lot of money;
- a committed and informed group of workers who knew what they had to do, so they didn't waste time trying to figure it out;
- A design group that was thereby able to deliver on time;
- A client-facing group that was able to deal with clients from a position of strength because they knew what stage each process was in. They kept the clients happy, and they didn't lose hundreds of thousands of dollars because a client or two got frustrated and took their business elsewhere.

These are the outcomes of Richard's work. They were impressive and he was able to sell himself confidently when he was interviewed. Even he was impressed with himself!

So now not only did Richard contribute to the bottom line in measurable ways, but he showed his leadership strengths. Indeed he would make a very well rounded, experienced VP who not only could lead but could understand the issues his project managers would face and be able to help them achieve the company's goals.

HERE IS YOUR JEWISH MOTHER COACH'S ADVICE FOR STEPPING UP INTO YOUR TALENTS AND STANDING OUT:

1. Make a list of the outcomes you delivered, NOT the responsibilities you had (although those are important).

2. Write out how each outcome helped the organization. If you can quantify it in terms of dollars, do that. If you can put it into percentages; e.g., the department's output now is 30% greater than it was last quarter; that's good too.

3. Look back at your talents/skills page (Chapter III) and tie the outcomes to them. For example, if you made something run more efficiently, did you decrease overtime hours?

4. Keep asking yourself this question: *"What difference did it make that I was there?"*

*"Procrastination is, hands down,
our favorite form of self-sabotage."*
—*Alyce P. Cornyn-Selby*

Chapter 5

Stop With The Lists!

Procrastinate and Suffer!

So What Is It -You Have A Headache? Later Is Not Better

If you never procrastinate, you can skip this chapter. But, if you're like most of us, you need to read on.

Sometimes later IS better, but not very often. The more you wait, the more you usually sabotage yourself. The thing you are avoiding doing gets more difficult the longer you wait to do it. I know you know this. But it's only half the story. Here's the rest.

1. Lists are only useful when you can cross stuff off. Some people are attached to their lists and do indeed cross things off as they accomplish them. That's good list behavior. However, if your list keeps getting longer and very few things are crossed off, then keeping a list is a time-consuming *avoidance* technique. Your list is *designed* to help you NOT do things.

∽ ∾

If you love lists, then the trick is to make the list useful, to make it a tool for getting things done.

∽ ∾

When I work with a client who procrastinates, one of the first things we do is corral all the tasks that need doing and "time-box" them. That is, we select a reasonable date for accomplishing each task. When you see a date on your calendar, and set some reminder alerts, it often makes it easier to allocate the time necessary, because you've made a visual commitment to it. Sounds hokey, I know, but it really works.

For some, time-boxing just increases the anxiety of completing something, but that is not necessarily a bad thing. It's part of learning new behaviors for overcoming procrastination. Of course, if the anxiety produces paralysis, it's time to talk to someone.

2. Not doing something is a choice you've made. As soon as you say, I can't – or won't – do that today because there's so much else I have to do, you've made a choice. You're doing other things instead. That's a problem when you continually do it. The price is usually the loss of something. The loss of an opportunity, the loss of productive hours, the loss of sleep – you know what it is.

∽ ✑

*No matter what you tell yourself, you are the only one who knows for sure whether what you **are** doing is a way of **not** doing something else.*

∽ ✑

If you can acknowledge that you have made a choice not to do something, don't berate yourself about it. Just own up and move on. Don't contemplate your inaction. That's *really* a waste of time.

3. It is not easy to change chronic "procrastination behavior." Have you ever tried to change your golf swing? You know how hard it is. BUT, when the outcome is worth it to you, somehow you find a way to make the change. It is a matter of value and will.

∽ ✑

Change is difficult in any situation. It requires practice and a conscious effort to keep your eyes on the prize —overcoming the drive not to do what needs doing.

∽ ✑

Sometimes the reason we procrastinate is because we fear success and sometimes it's because we fear failure. These fears are real, and the work of conquering them is tough. I can assure you that it is worth the effort. When you beat the beast you free up so much energy you get more done in less time. Really.

I said it before and I'll say it again. Procrastination is a deep-rooted behavior and changing it requires practice,

practice, and practice. Even then we don't change it forever.

Not doing something because you have so much on your plate that you simply hide from the overload is the way-of-the-world these days. Most working people are on overload.

Mostly, we avoid doing something until there is a deadline, we're being nagged, or we suddenly get motivated. The result of this kind of procrastination is external – that is someone else is waiting for something from us and they get angry if we don't produce. Here's the key to knowing if it's just normal unhelpful behavior or something deeper.

∽ ∾

The personal result of your procrastination is the difference between ordinary procrastination and paralysis.

∽ ∾

If you can handle the wrath you may produce without getting "wiggy", and you eventually do it, then it's likely normal procrastination. Clearly, if you do it a lot, you will be seen as someone who is **"gornish helfen"** (no help at all). And even though it's normal procrastination, it could lead you out the door! This is when it might be a good idea to get a coach to help you get over it as much as possible.

It becomes a deeper issue however, when the results of your procrastination lead to feeling badly about yourself most of the time – even when you're doing something enjoyable. It works something like this – you have something to do, you put it on a list, you likely never do it, but you just keep increasing the size of the list.

∽ ∾

Then you go around feeling like a loser most of the time.

∽ ∾

The result of your procrastination is internal to the point of paralysis. That's when it's time to see a shrink, not a coach. A coach may be able to help you get clear, such as was the case with Jason whose story is below. But to really address this kind of vicious circle – *I procrastinate and feel badly about myself because I procrastinate* – a good therapist is probably your best bet.

Chapter 5

Client Story

JASON

"I check my task list every day, and every day it seems to get longer with less done than the day before. I need someone to keep me on task and help me accomplish some of this stuff so that the list shrinks, not expands." This was Jason's cry for help to me.

First we looked at his task list. It was so long and so intense that no one could ever accomplish - ever - all the items on that list. It included professional, personal, family, and other tasks to be accomplished. So, the first job was to understand what was on the list and why it was there.

The next job was to help Jason gain an understanding of his own habits. Continuing to put things on his list was his way of kidding himself he would get to them when in fact it was a sure way not to get to them.

We also had to recognize that Jason's difficulty was deep-seated and would probably require some psychological intervention. Although he agreed that maybe at some point he might need to do some deeper work, other than coaching, he wasn't ready to give in to it yet.

The task therefore was to help him do two things. First, it was important for Jason to recognize that not doing something because he was doing something else was in fact a *choice* he was making. Second, so far as possible, we had to help him see his task list a little more creatively.

Jason was extremely dependent on his list. And he became very agitated when I talked about the possibility of doing away with it. So we decided to make the list more of a tool than a burden.

First, we separated the tasks into categories and we color-coded them. One color for professional things, another for family things, and so on. Then, we gave them a priority code. This would not automatically produce a behavior change, but it did give him a picture that allowed him to see separation and volume instead of one huge conglomeration of things. Since Jason was an engineer, the visual image turned out to be extremely useful to him.

We also looked at his list in terms of weeks and months, rather than days. With each task, I walked Jason through the elements involved in completing the task and we put more realistic time frames around them.

We spoke several times a week to go over the task list and to eliminate the tasks he actually accomplished. We moved things around within the list to reflect a more realistic position. By sticking with it, and following the pattern we established, Jason was able to recognize how deep his problem was. That gave him the courage to do something about it He did eventually seek psychological help because he could see that the fancy task list and phone calls to me were only temporary fixes.

IF YOU'RE A PROCRASTINATOR, HERE IS YOUR JEWISH MOTHER COACH'S ADVICE:

1. Ask yourself if the task to be accomplished is worth it. Answer the question.

2. Then admit it - putting it off is a choice, so don't make excuses for not doing it.

3. Remember, it takes time and practice to change behavior. Don't berate yourself for not doing it, just recognize that you have chosen to avoid it.

4. Do the hard things first. The longer you play around with the easy things, the difficult things begin to loom larger and larger until they are burdens and not tasks.

5. Break the task into steps if you have to, and TIME BOX everything
   a. Decide on the 3 things you WILL do.
   b. TIME BOX each of the three - Decide on when you will work on it (date and time) and keep the date.
   c. Decide to finish it.

6. Use some tools to help you. E.g., Fancy lists; alarm clocks to time yourself; designating a particular hour for working on it; talking into a recorder instead of writing it out.

7. If you think your procrastination issues are deeper than normal, or they stem from some paralyzing fear, get some help.

"Even if you are on the right track –
you'll get run over if you just sit there."
—Will Rogers

Chapter 6

Why Wouldn't Everybody Love You?

Managing Up and Managing Down

IS IT UP OR DOWN?

Successfully managing your bosses – managing up – and your staff – managing down - takes self-awareness, ingenuity, an ability to really hear what goes on within your company, and good communications.

The two most important elements of successfully managing in either direction are:

1. Communications – speaking the same language as your boss, helping your staff to understand your language, and communicating regularly
2. Building strong relationships.

Everyone has an agenda. It's as important to understand your boss's agenda and how he talks about it, as it is know your own and your staff's. Knowing your boss's style is essential in being able to manage his expectations. Of course, you need to know your own style as well so that you can calibrate or adjust to meet his needs without going into a tailspin.

For example, your boss may be looking for a promotion, and needing good numbers from your group to get that promotion. As a result, your boss may start demanding things, pushing you and your team unreasonably, and micromanaging.

What can you do? Your job is to help your boss succeed. This means finding what level of communication he needs and what's important to him. You also must be in charge of your time and your staff while helping him get that promotion. And to do that effectively, you have to manage his expectations. Managing his expectations will be much easier if you are proactive in communicating information. You have to tell him what kind of information he can expect and how that will help him do whatever it is he wants to do.

Now I don't mean you collude, or lie, or plot. What I do mean is that you need to genuinely understand what is important to your boss, how you can help him, and what you can provide to make him feel that he has some control.

If his demands become excessive, it is up to you to push back and to provide an alternative. Successfully managing up means you provide solutions, not problems. But, in managing up, the mantra is "it's about them, not about me." Self-awareness and ingenuity are the rules here. Recognizing – or hearing – what is important to the other person is the key to maintaining a mutually respectful relationship.

*You cannot change a person's characteristics –
you can only help them get what they need*

If managing up means managing expectations, then managing down, for the most part, means managing processes. The best way to manage processes is to be a coach. It's your job to see that the work of your unit is done effectively. Honestly caring about the people who are doing the work is the most powerful way to create a successful team. And a successful team is one that does the job well with a minimum of fuss.

Yes, you must also set expectations for the staff. But the difference is that your staff has to do the job you want done. Primarily, your job is to see that they have the tools, the access, and the means to do it. You need to provide the encouragement and regular communications they need to get the work done, all the while creating strong relationships and loyalty. Involving them in *how* things will get accomplished is the most effective way to get what you need.

The Carrot and the Stick

In the case of managing up, the carrots are that you will give your boss what s/he needs and that s/he can count on you to provide solutions. The stick is that you won't communicate enough for him or her to feel secure in what you're giving. Your boss needs to trust you. Be sure not to present surprises. If something happens that was not expected, it's up to you to find the way to present it and to suggest solutions.

In the case of managing down, the carrots are that staff members are involved in determining the process, and that they are cared about and respected by you. Also, they have some control over their destinies within your organization. The stick is that you will be evaluating their performances. I know that sounds crass, but it is the reality.

Most people want to do a good job. Your role is to help them do that by successfully managing the processes that produce their deliverables.

I don't want to scare you, but it's important to recognize that:

∽ ∾

Successfully navigating the political terrain of your organization is one of the most difficult challenges in the working world.

∽ ∾

Keep your eyes on the prize: in this case, it's having control over your work life. If you remember that communications and relationships are the keys, you will be golden.

Chapter 6

Client Story

JACK

Jack was COO of the largest division within a global conglomerate. Big job, right? The financial goals for Jack's division were steep but he met or exceeded them every quarter. He was able to do this by asking his managers to work very hard – some said unrealistically hard – and they in turn asked a lot of their respective staffs. Long hours and working weekends were frequent and led to grumbling and unhappiness among staff members.

While his Division Director was very happy with the results, he was critical of how Jack was managing his staff. The Division Director began to micromanage Jack by insisting on a daily update on all activity within Jack's division. Of course, tension, distrust and resentment grew between Jack and his Division Director.

So now Jack had two serious issues: 1) How to change the relationship between himself and his Division Director; and 2) How to change the work environment for his managers and their staffs.

As I described in this chapter, navigating the political terrain of your organization is one of the most difficult challenges in the working world. Doing it successfully is a hard-hat job!

Meeting or exceeding the numbers was a very positive thing for him, his DD, and the organization. But the unhappiness within his organization was troubling enough to his Director that, despite the numbers, he felt he had to involve himself in the daily operation of Jack's division. Disgruntled employees do not reflect well on any organization.

Jack's job in this case was to manage his boss's *expectations* and manage his managers' *processes* - and they required different approaches. Both efforts had to be consistent with the political culture of the organization.

His DD was not going to give up his micromanagement entirely, and certainly not right away. It was Jack's responsibility to help his boss develop confidence that he (Jack) was aware of the situation and was going to take care of it in a positive way. It took time and patience. Jack started by having a regular meeting with his DD to discuss the situation – and it was the only thing on the agenda. If his boss wanted to talk about something else in addition, it had to wait until the end of the primary discussion.

During that meeting, Jack assured his DD that he was aware of the situation. He had three issues to discuss and they were:

1.   His plan for dealing with it;
2.   Why he was not willing to deliver less than expected numbers; and,
3.   That it sometimes took extra work to meet the financial goals.

He asked his DD to give him 30-45 days to put the plan in place and promised that he would brief the DD every 2 weeks on the progress. He asked that the Director not call him every day; he asked for his trust, and he reassured him that he knew what the consequences could be if he didn't fix the problem.

Jack's candor and his thoughtfulness allowed his boss to give him the benefit of the doubt. He briefed the Director on the plan, asked for his suggestions and left the meeting having regained his stature as the COO in charge of his operation. By owning up, recognizing everyone's stake in the outcome, and developing a plan to take care of the problem – which included updating the Division Director regularly – he changed the expectations.

He then met with his managers, and revealed that word of his employees' unhappiness was beginning to reach the top layer. Jack explained that he wanted the work processes to change but they still had to meet or exceed the goals given to them. He wanted each of them to meet with their staffs for a brainstorming session on how they could change things to create a positive work environment.

The managers and Jack took all the suggestions, worked them into a plan, met with each group again to get final input, and then sent out a draft of the proposal. There was a final all-hands meeting where they unveiled the new approach. Jack had a flow chart made up so that the managers and the staffs could watch the progress toward the end date (30-45 days hence).

Jack asked the managers to tell their staffs that this was a genuine opportunity to have some control over their own destinies within the work place. He wanted them to be clear that it was a serious undertaking and their participation was necessary for a successful outcome. While some staff members believed it was just manipulation, most believed it was a true effort to make things better. Their participation was the talk of the entire company and they came up with what turned out to be a prototype for other divisions.

Jack's Division Director did cut back on the daily phone calls, but his style was such that he had to micro-manage something. Recognizing that this was indeed his style, Jack kept his interference under control by continually assuring him he would be kept informed of whatever was happening within his Division. This was the carrot. The stick of course was to *not* keep him informed as much as he wanted. Another way of managing expectations.

Jack's managers recognized that he would get involved in the daily operations if he needed to and he would make changes if the managers didn't stay on top of things. The carrot: staying out of the way. The stick : not staying out of the way.

Managing up and managing down – it's a full time job in itself.

MANAGE UP AND DOWN WITH YOUR JEWISH MOTHER COACH'S ADVICE:

1. Recognize that everyone has an agenda – bosses and subordinates. <u>Your job is to understand them</u>

2. Be clear about your own agenda. Ask and answer: <u>"what do I want"</u> – (e.g., going for the next level; outperforming another division; being seen as a leader; tripling your year-end profits.)

3. Identify those players with whom you have to interact.

4. Identify what's important to them and how they react to various circumstances within the organization. Know their language! "What do they want/need and how can I help them?"
   <u>This is THE necessary ingredient for successfully achieving your own goals and agenda.</u>

5. Keep a note pinned up on your computer: "Communicating; Relationships" so you don't forget. Find as many opportunities as you can to do both.

6. Managing up or down requires understanding the political terrain of your organization. This is complex and often risky. The best advice I can give you is to get a coach to help you do this successfully.

You expected something else?

*"Prejudice, not being founded on reason,
cannot be removed by argument."*
—*Samuel Johnson.*

Chapter 7

Play Nice!

When you Encounter Prejudice

DO THE RIGHT THING

It's easy to say that the right thing is to publicly confront prejudice when you are a victim of it or when you see others being victimized. But let me say right up front that while 1) prejudice anywhere is wrong and 2) it is true we all have an obligation to confront prejudice wherever we see it, it is often not easily addressed in the workplace.

If we happen to be in charge of someone's destiny in the workplace, it is vitally important that we make decisions based on performance and not on race, religion, gender, or other superficial aspects.

In this chapter, I am going to deal with the harsh realities of prejudice in the workplace. What are your real alternatives, regardless of your core beliefs?

What is The Motive?

If you are being treated unfairly, it is not necessarily prejudice. Life is often not fair. Your job is to sort out whether it's benign unfairness – that someone is just not that into you or your work – or something deeper.

∽ ⌒

It's not simple to sort out prejudice from mere dislike, and it is very difficult to prove prejudice.

∽ ⌒

Unfortunately, you sometimes will have to endure a number of unfair situations before you can determine if prejudice is involved. You need to ask why things are unfolding the way they are. Is it because you really aren't qualified for the task? Is it because someone else has been waiting a long time for the recognition? Is it because you don't really work well with someone else? Or is it prejudice?

If, after enough hurtful events, you truly believe you are a victim of prejudice, what's the first thing you have to do? ADMIT IT to yourself.

∽ ⌒

I am talking here about a deep recognition of discrimination – of being told in countless ways that you are not good enough because you are the wrong color, the wrong religion, the wrong sex, the wrong look. It is painful and sometimes debilitating.

∽ ↝

When you have regained your equilibrium, you need to think through your options. There are basically three: you can confront it, report it, or ignore it. Each of these three actions has a number of elements you must consider before taking any decisive action.

OPTION 1: CONFRONT IT
This is the courageous and moral action to take. It also has several potentially disastrous consequences, so be sure you're ready for them.

First, be ready for outrage. If you get that reaction you know you've hit a nerve.

Be ready for word to spread that you are a troublemaker.

Be ready for your colleagues to avoid you – and know that this pain is even worse than the pain of admitting it.

∽ ↝

You may not change a thing outwardly. That is, everything stays the same except you are now not thought of as a team player. You never were, and that is why you did what you did.

∽ ↝

What you will have is the knowledge that you did the right thing and withstood the blows. If you choose this action – bravo! – be sure you are ready for the potential consequences.

AND BTW, it may turn out really well. This is a gift.

Option 2: Report It

This is also the courageous and right thing to do.

∽ ⌒

The first thing about this is to identify the right person to report it to. It may not be HR; it may be the CEO.

∽ ⌒

The downside? The same issues as in confronting it apply here as well. It may take a little longer to go public, but when it does you may be in for the same consequences. Again, it may work out really well, but my advice is to be prepared if it doesn't – which is far more likely.

Option 3: Ignore it

You (and I) will take a lot of flack for this option. I am not recommending it. I am being realistic about the fact that it happens and letting you all know that I know. I've done it and I've been a victim of it.

We have all kinds of rationalizations for ignoring it – I'll be ostracized by the team; I can't rock the boat because I want that promotion – whatever. You can tell yourself anything and it will be your reason. You need to do what is best for you. You will have to deal with your conscience, however. If you can withstand your own heat, and it is the better part of valor for your future, then recognize it as such and move on.

No one has the only perspective on the right thing to do. There are many issues that come into play for each individual.

⤳ ⤶

Your job is to be as honest as you can
be and to do what seems best to you.

⤳ ⤶

It would be wonderful if we could all always be righteous and denounce prejudice openly under all circumstances. But sometimes we just can't. The trick is to be honest with yourself about what you're doing, why you're doing it, and to be able to live with your own conscience.

As a Jewish person, I've been the victim of bigotry and prejudice from the time I was a child. It was always painful and it always shook my confidence in myself. Often, I chose to ignore the remarks, and sometimes I called them out – but only when I wasn't afraid I would lose something or someone. I did continue on with what I knew was the right path for me despite the pain. I'm not proud of the fact that I allowed people to get away with it, but I no longer sweep such things under the rug. It has not always been easy, or pleasant and it's something I live with everyday.

As a child of about 6 or 7 I had a best friend who lived next door. We walked to school together, played together, and had mutual other friends from my block. I really loved him – in a 6-year-old's way and only as a friend. One day he came to my back door and pounded on it. I opened and he screamed "I can't play with you anymore you killed Jesus!" I burst into tears proclaiming I had never killed anyone and he just had to be my best friend, he just had to be! He turned and ran home.

I begged my mother to talk with his mother and tell her we didn't kill anyone and it was ok for him to continue to be my friend. She said something like "those people aren't worth talking to just ignore it. You'll find another best friend."

I had so much to think about that I cried and couldn't sleep for weeks. I learned two things that day, that Jews were disliked (hated is more like it) and that fear of confronting people was turned into reverse prejudice. I became very sensitive to prejudice in others and in myself as well. It was why I was able to hone in on the issue in the client story below so quickly. I know the drill intimately.

Growing up I often didn't confront anyone when I was the victim of that prejudice, or let on that I was a Jew when I heard slurs. I would just take my pain and either talk to another Jewish friend about them, or rationalize why it was ok that I didn't speak up. I no longer do that. I will speak up every time.

Finding ways to cope with this choice is not easy. Some of us work for the rights of others to make up for it; some of us pray for forgiveness; some of us vow to raise our children free of racial and gender prejudice; and I'm sure you can think of other ways. Perhaps you have your own.

When we choose to ignore it because we're afraid, or we think we may lose something, we do. We may not lose the job, or the contract, or the argument, but we do lose a piece of ourselves. It is always there. We just get really good at burying it. I no longer ignore it but I don't judge those who do. It isn't admirable but it is human.

❧ ❧

If this is what you choose, the most important thing is to be honest with yourself.

❧ ❧

Chapter 7

Client Story

RENAY

An experienced and highly qualified health care provider, Renay was having difficulty communicating with her peers and her supervisors. When she suggested changes for her department – which she did at departmental meetings where such suggestions were encouraged – she was met with skepticism about her ideas and condescending remarks about her ability to deal with issues. Renay is from the middle east.

She took all the necessary first steps. She asked to speak one-on-one with her supervisor and told her how she felt. The supervisor assured her that no one was trying to marginalize her or her contributions, essentially dismissing Renay's experiences.

She talked one-on-one with her colleagues who, in varying degrees, dismissed her concerns, but said they would be more mindful of her feelings in the future.

In fact, things got worse. Renay was now completely ignored at the departmental meetings, and her colleagues avoided any discussions with her except when necessary to discuss her patients. The final blow came when she was passed over for a promotion that she clearly deserved and which had been promised by the executive director. It was given to someone who was far less qualified.

When we spoke, Renay was trying to find new ways to talk with her fellow practitioners, and she wanted help to see her situation in an unemotional and logical way. We spoke for quite awhile and then I told her that the question I was about to ask would be difficult and hurtful but it had to be asked: "Renay, do you think any of this is due to unspoken prejudice?" She began to cry and said, "Yes".

She had been working very hard to fit in and become just one of the crew. Here is the hard truth: **if prejudice, racism, sexism, or any other kind of bigotry is practiced and supported silently, there is no way the victim of such behavior can win.** And it was certainly true in Renay's case.

Renay struggled because she was trying to give her colleagues the benefit of the doubt while also being true to herself. Admirable indeed. However, there comes a point when a decision has to be made, and Renay had reached that point.

Renay's real alternatives were: to report her situation to the administration and or the Board; to call out the behaviors when they happen; to leave the organization; or to try to find other opportunities within the organization.

Before any choice could be made, Renay had to struggle with her own recognition that she was indeed a victim of racism. This turned out to be the most difficult part of her ability to take the next steps. The hurt was so deep and so profound that rescuing herself seemed beyond her control.

After soul-searching, and some positive reinforcement from her family, friends, and her coach, she made the decision to leave, but to tell the administration and the Board why she made that decision.

What happened? Renay talked with the CEO and the Board Chairperson to describe her experience and to explain her reason for leaving. They were sympathetic, seemed to be appalled, told her they would certainly investigate, but there was no attempt to keep her – to ask her to stay.

We can speculate endlessly on why, particularly since she had such an excellent reputation for her medical and patient care skills, but we will never really know.

Renay got another position as head of the emergency department at another hospital and is doing very well. My regret is that I haven't spoken with her since the event so I don't know how the experience changed her – or even if it did. I hope it changed all of them.

IF YOU ARE IN THE UNHAPPY CIRCUMSTANCE OF HAVING TO DEAL WITH PREJUDICE, EXCESSIVE BIAS OR UNFAIRNESS, HERE IS YOUR JEWISH MOTHER COACH'S ADVICE:

1. The first thing you have to do when you observe or encounter bias or prejudice is to ADMIT IT to yourself.

2. Decide if you are going to confront it, report it, or ignore it.

3. Talk with someone outside and with no stake in the situation before you take any action.

4. Weigh the many factors associated with each of these actions.

5. Be honest about your threshold for backlash including your own conscience.

6. Learn something about yourself from the experience.

Conclusion

Here are the three things this Jewish Mother Coach hopes you will take away from this little guide – (besides doing what I tell you).

First – No matter what you face, you're not alone. Many others have dealt with that very thing and come through just fine. The key is to honestly examine yourself first, and talk to someone who cares about you, preferably a Jewish Mother type. BTW, men can be Jewish Mother types too.

Second – Be a **"mentsh"** (an admirable person) even when you have to be strategic. A person's gotta do what a person's gotta do, right? Just do it so your own conscience is intact.

Third – Be smarter next week than you were this week and if you need help doing that, get it.

So maybe you could write or call once in a while, just to let me know what you think and how you're doing? I really would love to hear from you – whatever you have to say.

Thanks for listening and, finally – the most important advice of all – *just do what I tell you!*

Here are all the ways you can connect with me:
Emails: ruth@thejewishmothercoach.com or ruth@mottcoaching.com

http://www.facebook.com/mottcoaching
http://www.twitter.com/mottcoaching
http://www.linkedin.com/in/ruthmott
http://thejewishmothercoach.com

Suggested Reading

My recommended reading includes literature as well as business books. While business books are useful, I believe that reading literature broadens one's view of the world in a more personal way. And I also believe that our personal views exert the strongest influence on our professional behaviors. There are many wonderful books out there and these are just a few of my favorites.

The Answer to How is Yes: Acting on What Matters by PETER BLOCK, Berrett-Koehler pub. This is one of the best out there in my opinion. If something is truly important the real question is "why" not "how". Asking "why" frees your creativity and your capacity to truly change things. It works in business and in your personal life as well.

The Protean Self: Human Resilience in An Age of Fragmentation by ROBERT JAY LIFTON, University of Chicago Press pub. The hectic pace of our time and the multi-tasking necessary to stay afloat cause anxiety and fear that we won't be able to cope. In this book, Dr. Lifton shows how we are able to invent and reinvent ourselves by controlling the barrage of forces we face everyday.

Moby Dick by HERMAN MELVILLE, Multiple pubs. This classic tale demonstrates, like few others, how powerful instinct can overtake the best-laid strategies. As a coach I often work with clients to develop their strategic abilities. And then I caution them to listen to their instincts.

Books by NICK MORGAN: Read all of them, they are excellent. You will find them at Amazon.com and at www.publicwords.com

Trust Me: Four Steps to Authenticity and Charisma
Give Your Speech, Change The World;
The King's Speech, Lessons for Leaders
How to Tell Great Business Stories
How to Read Body Language
7 Steps to a Great Speech

The Zen of Listening: Mindful Communication In The Age of Distraction by REBECCA Z. SHAFIR, Quest Books pub. Listening is the key to success both professionally and personally. This book eloquently explains how to do that so you can build trust, strengthen your relationships, and increase your concentration.

Plays of WILLIAM SHAKESPEARE, Multiple pubs. Reading a few of the plays is just a good thing to do – period. It broadens your literacy and, if you pay close attention, you will see that he comes at each play with a fresh mind. He lets the story define the characters and the plots. This is extremely useful if you are writing, giving a presentation, or need to clear your head so you can be into the next game.

Rules of Thumb: 52 Truths for Winning at Business without Losing Yourself by ALAN W WEBBER, Harper Business pub. One of the best how-to books I've read. It's clear, concise, and courageous. It really does give you the road map and specific tools. It contains 52 practical lessons gleaned from 40 years of working with leaders. It's a small book packed with really useful stuff.

Leadership and the New Science: Discovering Order in a Chaotic World by MARGARET J. WHEATLEY, Barrett-Koehler pub. By using the breakthroughs in biology, chemistry, and even physics, Wheatley gives you a new way to think about organizations and your places in them.

Poetry – yes Poetry. I often use Poetry to help my clients hone their critical thinking skills. By reading poetry, then thinking through (out loud is best) what the message is, you begin to develop your own thoughts about whatever the message is and can articulate it more clearly. The more clarity you have about your ideas, the ideas of others, and the various ways messages can be relayed, the more value you can add to any group or organization. BTW, reading poetry can also help bring you some breathing room to simply get in touch with your own thoughts. This is not a bad thing.

Two of my favorites:

The Poetry of Robert Frost – Henry Holt and Company, pub.

A Book of Luminous Things: An International Anthology of Poetry byCZESLAW MILOSZ, Harcourt Brace pub.

Short Bio

Ruth Mott has over 18 years experience as an Executive Coach helping individuals and organizations identify, expand, and achieve their visions.

Her unique skill lies in coaching executives, consultants, and others in communicating their knowledge, passions and wisdom; helping them change behaviors enabling them to achieve and contribute to their maximum capabilities.

Ruth has worked across a broad range of businesses - from electronics to colleges; from television to global corporations. Her direct and open style helps her clients make very quick progress, inspire others and implement action and change.

"My multifaceted background has significantly contributed to my abilities and success as an executive coach. More than anything, my experience has taught me how to be a truly helpful partner *for my clients. "*

In addition to her work in the United States, Ruth has worked in Ireland, England, Germany, Belgium, and Portugal.

19414073R00060

Made in the USA
Middletown, DE
19 April 2015